Are Names Important?

Names are very important to God. So important that sometimes he even changed them. There are a lot of baby name books out there, but David Brown thought, "Why not one for Christians?" He's done a great job of compiling these names in *A is for Adam, E is for Eve* and given us a fresh and deeper look into the Word of God. Thanks David!

—*Karen J. Sanders–Aide for the elderly and disadvantaged*

I enjoyed *A is for Adam, E is for Eve*. Are names important? Very much! I found the book interesting and informative. It will be an extremely helpful guide for families wanting to use biblical names for their children.

—*Barbara Kennedy–Mother of three*

This handbook of names for babies is a nice addition to your library. It tells the meaning of the names and also gives some information about that person. A thoughtful undertaking for a first-time journalist.

—Ernestine Saunders–Mature, wise, and faithful Christian woman

An interesting collection of mid-eastern names that will allow you to pick one for your newborn to wear with pride.

—Angyla Faust–Housewife in Nashville, Tennessee

People who want to get back to their roots will be interested in these biblical names!

—Elizabeth McDonald–Carnegie Mellon graduate

A is for Adam
E is for Eve

DAVID BROWN

A is for Adam
E is for Eve

A Biblical Guide for Naming Your Child

TATE PUBLISHING & Enterprises

A is for Adam, E is for Eve
Copyright © 2009 by David Brown. All rights reserved.

Scripture quotations marked "NASU" are taken from the *New American Standard Bible Update,* Copyright © 1960, 1962, 1963, 1968, 1971, 1972, 1973, 1975, 1977, 1995 by The Lockman Foundation. Used by permission. All rights reserved.

Scripture quotations marked "NKJV" are taken from *The New King James Version* / Thomas Nelson Publishers, Nashville: Thomas Nelson Publishers. Copyright © 1982. Used by permission. All rights reserved.

Scripture quotations marked "NIV" are taken from the *Holy Bible, New International Version* ®, Copyright © 1973, 1978, 1984 by International Bible Society. Used by permission of Zondervan Publishing House. All rights reserved.

Pronunciations of the names are included in parentheses and are taken from YourDictionary.com.

Meanings of names are included in italics and are taken from BehindtheName.com.

The opinions expressed by the author are not necessarily those of Tate Publishing, LLC.

Published by Tate Publishing & Enterprises, LLC
127 E. Trade Center Terrace | Mustang, Oklahoma 73064 USA
1.888.361.9473 | www.tatepublishing.com

Tate Publishing is committed to excellence in the publishing industry. The company reflects the philosophy established by the founders, based on Psalm 68:11,
"The Lord gave the word and great was the company of those who published it."

Book design copyright © 2009 by Tate Publishing, LLC. All rights reserved.
Cover & interior design by Lindsay B. Behrens

Published in the United States of America

ISBN: 978-1-60799-089-5
Family & Relationships / Baby Names
09.04.20

Dedication

A is for Adam, E is for Eve is dedicated to the expecting Christians of the world. May this book guide and help you in making an educated decision when naming your baby. Your child will thank you for it later. Take care and God bless.

Acknowledgments

First of all, I would like to express my gratitude to God (who happens to be the real author of this book anyway). Also, I would like to thank my mom, Delaine, for supporting me throughout this process; the staff at Tate Publishing, who have helped turn a manuscript into a fun and helpful book; and last but certainly not least: Tom and Debbie Yeager, Karen Sanders, Seth Nuthak, and Jeff Taylor, the Bible scholars and experienced Christians who edited, expanded upon, and then double- and triple-checked the biblical information in this book.

Foreword

Two weeks before my fortieth birthday, God blessed my husband and me with a second beautiful baby boy. I named him David after the biblical David, whom I had always admired for his closeness to God and many writings.

This book David has penned will help you find and decide on a name for your little blessing.

May you love and enjoy each child,

—Delaine Brown

Introduction

> He who has an ear, let him hear what the Spirit says to the churches. To him who overcomes, to him I will give *some* of the hidden manna, and I will give him a white stone, and a new name written on the stone which no one knows but he who receives it.
>
> Revelation 2:17 (NASU)

Are names important? Yes, they are. Some may say that a name is just a word, but we know there's one word that's more important than anything else in existence. John 1:1: "In the beginning was the Word, and the Word was with God, and the Word was God" (NIV).

As if that weren't enough, God himself created names when he chose the word Adam for his first human instead of just calling him "man." Furthermore, in the book of Genesis, we can see the importance names were given since Adam's first job was to name things. Genesis 2:19 reads: Out of the ground the LORD God formed every beast of the field and every bird of the sky, and brought them to the man to see what he would call them; and whatever the man called a living creature, that was its name" (NASU).

Not long after, God has Adam naming his new partner. "The man said, 'This is now bone of my bones, And flesh of my flesh; She shall be called Woman, Because she was taken out of Man'" (Genesis 2:23, NASU).

God uses names all the time. In the New American Standard Updated version of the Bible, the word "name" is used 866 times—from Genesis to Revelations. The last two examples of the importance of names are as follows: "And if anyone's name was not found written in the book of life, he was thrown into the lake of fire" (Revelations 20:15), and "There will no longer be any curse; and the throne of God and of the Lamb will be in it, and His bondservants will serve Him; they will see His face, and His name *will be* on their foreheads. And there will no longer be any night; and they will not have need of the light of a lamp nor the light of the sun, because the Lord God will illumine them; and they will reign forever and ever" (Revelations 22:3–5).

Here are some steps to remember when selecting a name for your child.

- First, as you read through the book, make a list of the names that you see and like. (If you don't know the gender of your child, make a separate list for boys and girls.)

- Second, read the meanings of the names and the descriptions of the people you have selected to get a better view of who they were.

- Third, eliminate the namesakes that aren't your favorites.

- Fourth, review the remaining list. If you would like, use the Scripture references to research a more in-depth story about the people on your list.

- Fifth, continue to narrow the list down, so that you have only two or three names left.

- Sixth, ask family and friends what they think about the names on your list.

- Seventh, giving your own opinion the most weight, choose the name you like the best.

May your child grow to follow in the footsteps of the name you have chosen.

נֶסהגֻ_שׁאַה_ּיֶ_מאַנֶ_הת שׂ סֶפֶתסֶתשׂ_הת נֶ וּלֶלשׂ ּת ורג דֶלֶהצ רֶּי יאַם

Sincerely,

—David Brown

> He found first his own brother Simon and said to him, "We have found the Messiah" (which translated means Christ). He brought him to Jesus. Jesus looked at him and said, "You are Simon the son of John; you shall be called Cephas" (which is translated Peter).
>
> John 1:41–42 (NASU)

Names for Boys

Abram fell on his face, and God talked with him, saying, "As for Me, behold, My covenant is with you, And you will be the father of a multitude of nations. No longer shall your name be called Abram, But your name shall be Abraham; For I will make you the father of a multitude of nations."

Genesis 17:3–5 (NASU)

** People continually failing or strongly against God.

* People who failed God, were punished in a severe way, or weren't Christian.

⁺⁺ One of the three most righteous named by Ezekiel.

¹² One of the twelve apostles of Jesus.

Note that a minor prophet is no less important than a major prophet; it only means they wrote less in the Bible.

The letters YHWH represent the unspoken name of God as gifted to the Jews. God restricted the use of this name for special purposes only; furthermore, it is not found in any of the English translations of the Bible.

A

*Aaron: (er′ən, ar′ən) *high mountain or exalted:* The older brother of Moses by three years. Aaron assisted Moses as his public speaker and prophet. After fleeing the slavery of Egypt, the Lord appointed Aaron and his decedents to serve him as priests. However, he failed God when he gave in to the people's wishes to worship a golden calf at Mount Sinai. NASU, NKJV, *and* NIV *Chapters:* Exodus 4–12, 16–19, 24, 27–32, 34, 35, 38–40; Leviticus 1–3, 6–11, 13–17, 21, 22, 24; Numbers 1–4, 6–10, 12–20, 25–27, 33; Deuteronomy 9, 10; Psalm 105, 106; and Acts 7.

Abel: (ā′bəl) *breath:* Adam and Eve's second son. Abel chose to be a shepherd and was killed by his older brother, Cain, a farmer. This was because the Lord had regard for Abel's offering and none for Cain's. NASU, NKJV, *and* NIV *Chapters:* Genesis 4; Hebrews 11.

Abraham: (ā′brə ham′) *father of many:* He lived as a faithful servant of God, and he's included in the genealogy of Jesus. Abraham was tested severely by God for most of his life and succeeded; therefore, God rewarded him. He was around one hundred years old when the reward included his first child, a healthy boy. NASU, NKJV, *and* NIV *Chapters:* Genesis 17–26; Mathew 1, 8; Mark 12; Luke 16; and Galatians 3.

Abram: (ā′brəm) *high father:* Abraham's first name before God changed it. When the Lord told the seventy-five-year-old Abram to leave his home, family, and even his country to go to Egypt, he obeyed without complaint. NASU, NKJV, *and* NIV *Chapters:* Genesis 11–17; Nehemiah 9.

*Adam: (ad′əm) *man:* As the first man handcrafted by God, he named all the animals of the earth. Adam was exiled from the Garden of Eden and cursed to toil when he ate of the forbidden fruit. From the time God created him, Adam lived to be 930 years old. NASU, NKJV, *and* NIV *Chapters:* Genesis 2–5; 1 Chronicles 1.

*Alexander: (al'ig zan'dər) *defending men:* One was a high priest in Jerusalem who helped corner Peter and John for trial. **Another Alexander, who lived in Ephesus, was converted to Christianity by Paul before later losing his faith and conscience. NASU, NKJV, *and* NIV *Chapters:* Acts 4, 19; 1 Timothy 1.

Amos: (ā'məs) *to carry:* A herdsman and sycamore grower who became one of the great prophets made by God. Amos is listed in the genealogy of Jesus. After being instructed by the Lord, Amos was treated badly by Israel for proclaiming their corruption; however, he remained faithful throughout this ordeal. NASU, NKJV, *and* NIV *Chapters:* The book of Amos; Luke 3.

¹²Andrew: (an'droo') *of a man:* Andrew and his brother Simon, who was called Peter, were the first two people called by Jesus to become disciples. After Jesus had come down from praying on a mountain, He chose twelve disciples, one of whom was Andrew, to become apostles. NASU, NKJV, *and* NIV *Chapters:* Matthew 4, 10; Mark 1, 3; Luke 6; John 1, 6, 12; and Acts 1.

*Augustus: (ô gus′təs, ə gus′təs) *great:* Augustus was Caesar when Jesus was born. He created a time of stability in Rome, although he was not a Christian and did not favor them. NASU *and* NIV *Chapters:* Luke 2. NKJV *Differences:* Add Acts 25, which names the emperor as Augustus.

B

Barnabas: (bär′nə bəs) *son of encouragement:* Originally called Joseph, he was a Levite of Cyprian birth who the apostles called Barnabas. He was a hard-working Christian and put in charge of some important tasks for churches in different cities. This had him traveling a lot of the time with the Apostle Paul. NASU, NKJV, *and* NIV *Chapters:* Acts 4, 9, 11–15; Galatians 2.

[12]**Bartholomew:** (bär thäl′ə myoo′) *son of a deep and narrow groove:* There are only four times he is mentioned in the Bible: twice when Jesus chose the twelve apostles, once when the twelve were instructed to go out and preach Jesus to all of Israel, and finally in the upper room where Matthias was appointed to replace Judas Iscariot. Bartholomew faithfully kept to the work of an apostle. There are no poor actions written of him in the Bible. NASU, NKJV, *and* NIV *Chapters:* Matthew 10; Mark 3; Luke 6; and Acts 1.

Benjamin: (ben′jə mən) *son of the right hand:* The youngest son of Jacob, Benjamin was well loved by his father and his brother Joseph. This is possibly because out of eleven brothers, Benjamin was the only one who came from the same mother, Rachel. Also, he's the only brother who wasn't involved in the plot against Joseph. NASU, NKJV, *and* NIV *Chapters:* Genesis 35, 42, 43, 45, 46, 49; Exodus 1; 1 Chronicles 7 and 8.

C

Caleb: (kā′ləb) *dog:* From the tribe of Judah, he was one of the twelve spies sent to scout the Promised Land. Caleb stayed true to God, kept his faith against overwhelming odds, and was rewarded with the land of Hebron because of this. NASU, NKJV, *and* NIV *Chapters:* Numbers 13, 14, 26, 32, 34; Deuteronomy 1; Joshua 14, 15, 21; Judges 1; and 1 Chronicles 1.

Cornelius: (kôr nēl′yəs) *horn:* He was a Roman solder; a centurion of what was called the Italian cohort. An angel of God called to him and directed Cornelius to send some of his men to Joppa. There they were to find Simon, who was also called Peter, and ask him to return with them. This proved to Peter that God also wanted gentiles to be baptized into Christianity. NASU, NKJV, *and* NIV *Chapters:* Acts 10.

D

Dan: (dan) *he judged:* The son of Jacob and Rachel's maid Bilhah. Rachel named him this because she said, "God has vindicated me, and has indeed heard my voice and has given me a son" (Genesis 30:6, NASU). NASU, NKJV, *and* NIV *Chapters:* Genesis 30, 35, 46, 49; Exodus 1.

⁺⁺**Daniel:** (dan′yəl) *God is my judge:* Named by the prophet Ezekiel as one of the three most righteous people who ever lived. Daniel was also a priest, prophet, and a wise man who could interpret dreams. He was thrown into the lion's den and survived unscathed. NASU *and* NIV *Chapters:* The book of Daniel and Matthew 24. NKJV *Differences:* Add Mark 13 since it names the prophet as Daniel.

*David: (dā′vid) *beloved:* The greatest king of Israel. David slew Goliath as a youth and had many personas, including warrior, faithful friend, musician, rebel, shepherd, and model king. His flaw was his lust for women and the adultery he caused by it. NASU, NKJV, *and* NIV *Chapters:* Ruth 4; 1 Samuel 16–30; 2 Samuel 1–13, 15–24; and 1 Kings 1 and 2.

E

*Eli: (ē′lī′) *ascension:* A high priest and judge. Eli would not properly discipline his sons after receiving a warning from God; consequently, all of his sons were killed as punishment. After news of his last two sons' deaths, Eli fell down, broke his neck, and died. NASU, NKJV, *and* NIV *Chapters:* 1 Samuel 1–4.

Elijah: (ē lī′jə, i lī′jə) *my God is YHWH:* The head prophet of Israel. Elijah was named the greatest prophet of all the Jews. God allowed him to cause a drought and pray for fire to burn his water-soaked offering, thus revealing the folly of worshiping the false god baal. NASU, NKJV, *and* NIV *Chapters:* 1 Kings 17–19, 21; 2 Kings 1, 2; and 2 Chronicles 21.

Elisha: (ē lī′shə, i lī′shə) *my God is salvation:* The apprentice of Elijah. Elisha continued the work of a prophet for God after Elijah was taken into heaven by a whirlwind. NASU, NKJV, *and* NIV *Chapters:* 1 Kings 19; 2 Kings 2–9 and 13.

Esau: (ē'sô') *hairy:* The oldest son of Isaac. Esau was cheated by his younger brother, Jacob, twice. He was said to be very hairy, an outdoorsman, and an extremely successful hunter. NASU, NKJV, *and* NIV *Chapters:* Genesis 25–28, 32, 33, 35, and 36.

Ethan: (ē'thǝn) *solid, enduring:* Ethan the Ezrahite was one of the wisest men in Israel. His name was used as a comparison when describing King Solomon, whom God had blessed with more wisdom than three nations. Another Ethan, a Levite, was a renowned singer for King David. He was selected by David as one of the performers who would sing praises and play bronze cymbals as the Ark of the Covent was returned to Jerusalem. NASU, NKJV, *and* NIV *Chapters:* 1 Kings 4; 1 Chronicles 15.

G

Gabriel: (gā′brē əl) *strong man of God:* An angel who is a peaceful messenger of God. This angel provided Daniel with the meaning of a vision, starting with the words, "Son of man, understand that the vision concerns the time of the end" (Daniel 8:17, NIV). Also, one day while Zacharias was performing priestly incense duties in the temple, Gabriel appeared to him and said, "Do not be afraid, Zacharias, for your prayer is heard; and your wife Elizabeth will bear you a son, and you shall call his name John. And you will have joy and gladness, and many will rejoice at his birth. For he will be great in the sight of the Lord, and shall drink neither wine nor strong drink. He will also be filled with the Holy Spirit, even from his mother's womb. And he will turn many of the children of Israel to the Lord their God. He will also go before Him in the spirit and power of Elijah, 'to turn the hearts of the fathers to the children,' and the disobedient to the wisdom of the just, to make ready a people prepared for the Lord" (Luke 1:13–17, NKJV). And so the birth of John the Baptist was foretold. NASU, NKJV, *and* NIV *Chapters:* Daniel 8, 9; Luke 1.

Isaac: (ī′zək) *he laughs:* The son of Abraham. Isaac became wealthy in life and owned many herds of animals. He had two warring sons who later made peace with each other. Isaac lived a life of such faith that Jesus uses his name to the Jews when explaining who God is. "But regarding the resurrection of the dead, have you not read what was spoken to you by God: 'I AM THE GOD OF ABRAHAM, AND THE GOD OF ISAAC, AND THE GOD OF JACOB'? He is not the God of the dead but of the living" (Matthew 22:31–32, NASU). NASU, NKJV, *and* NIV *Chapters:* Genesis 17, 18, 21, 22, 24–28, 35; 1 Chronicles 1; Matthew 8; and Hebrews 11.

Isaiah: (ī zā′ə) *YHWH is salvation:* A prophet of God who mainly interacted with King Hezekiah. Isaiah received visions concerning the reigns of Kings Uzziah, Jotham, Ahaz, and Hezekiah and spoke for God many times as seen in the book of Isaiah. His prophecies from God are quoted and taught by Jesus and the apostles several times. These are found in the books of Matthew, Mark, Luke, John, Acts, and Romans. NASU, NKJV, *and* NIV *Chapters:* 2 Kings 19, 20; 2 Chronicles 26, 32; and the book of Isaiah.

J

Jacob: (jā′kəb) *supplanter:* Jacob stole his older brother's birthright and blessing. In turn, Jacob was tricked into marrying Leah instead of her younger sister. Late one night, Jacob wrestled with a "man" as written in the Bible. This being wouldn't tell Jacob his name; however, he was able to dislocate Jacob's hip with just a touch and bless him by saying, "Your name will no longer be Jacob, but Israel, because you have struggled with God and with men and have overcome" (Genesis 32:28, NIV). After the man left, Jacob called the place Peniel, saying, "It is because I saw God face to face, and yet my life was spared" (Genesis 32:30, NIV). Also, the name Jacob was used by God when he identified himself to Moses in Exodus 3:6. He said also, "I am the God of your father, the God of Abraham, the God of Isaac, and the God of Jacob." Then Moses hid his face, for he was afraid to look at God (NASU). NASU, NKJV, *and* NIV *Chapters:* Genesis 25, 27–35, 37, 42, 45–49; Exodus 1.

¹²James: (jāmz) *may God protect:* James was the son of Zebedee and a fisherman before becoming one of the twelve apostles of Jesus. Due to his harsh temper, Jesus nicknamed him and his brother John *Boanerges,* which means "Sons of Thunder." A different James was Jesus' physical brother. 12 Another, who was also one of the twelve and loved by Jesus, was James, the son of Alphaeus. NASU, NKJV, *and* NIV *Chapters:* Matthew 4, 10, 13, 17; Mark 1, 3, 5, 6, 9, 10, 13, 14; Luke 5, 6, 8, 9; Acts 1, 12, 15, 21; 1 Corinthians 1; Galatians 1, 2; and the book of James.

Jared: (jar'id) *descent:* As one of Adam's descendants through Seth, he was born when his father, Mahalalel, was sixty-five. Jared himself had his first child, a son named Enoch, when he was 162. Nothing was written of Jared except for his place in his family tree and the fact that he had sons and daughters. He is listed in the genealogy of Jesus and lived to the ripe old age of 962. NASU, NKJV, *and* NIV *Chapters:* Genesis 5; 1 Chronicles 1; and Luke 3.

Jason: (jā′sən) *to heal:* A convert to Christianity, Jason hid Paul in his house during a riot in Thessalonica that was directed toward Paul's teachings. It is likely that Jason continued helping Paul and was well known as a good and faithful person to many, since he is also mentioned in Paul's letter, which was written by Tertius to the Christians in Rome. NASU, NKJV, *and* NIV *Chapters:* Acts 17; Romans 16.

Jedidiah: (jed əh dī əh) *beloved of YHWH:* As the son of King David and Bathsheba, he was named Solomon. The Lord loved him and conveyed this to the prophet Nathan; therefore Solomon was named Jedidiah for the Lord's sake. He became king after his father and was blessed by God not only as the wisest man in his own country, but also with more wisdom than "all the sons of the east and all the wisdom of Egypt." NASU, NKJV, *and* NIV *Chapters:* 2 Samuel 12.

Jeremiah: (Jer' emī əh) *YHWH has uplifted:* Two are listed in King David's group of "mighty men." They were great warriors of strength, valor, and speed. Another Jeremiah was destined by God to be a prophet before his parents even conceived him. The Lord stretched out his hand and appointed this Jeremiah as a prophet when he was still just a youth. He was the prophet who foretold Jesus' betrayal for thirty pieces of silver. Three of his prophecies are mentioned in Daniel 9, Matthew 2, and Matthew 27. NASU, NKJV, *and* NIV *Chapters:* 1 Chronicles 12; the book of Jeremiah; and Lamentations 3.

Jesse: (jes'ē) *gift:* He was from the town of Bethlehem. Jesse had eight sons including King David to whom he was a devoted and loving father. After a forty-day standoff, as the Philistines prepared to invade Judah, Jesse sent David, his youngest, to bring his brothers in the war some food and return with news. Because of this, David had his famous battle with Goliath. Jesse is often mentioned as a root in the genealogy of Jesus. NASU, NKJV, *and* NIV *Chapters:* Ruth 4; 1 Samuel 16, 17; 1 Chronicles 2 and Matthew 1.

Joab: (jō'ab') *YHWH is father:* As the commander of Kind David's army, Joab was a very powerful and courageous man of strength. He fought in many battles and preformed various tasks for his king including suppressing civil strife and census taking. NASU, NKJV, *and* NIV *Chapters:* 2 Samuel 2, 3, 8, 10–12, 14, 18–20, 23, 24 1 Kings 1, 2; and 1 Chronicles 11, 18–21, and 27.

++Job: (jō'b') *persecuted:* Named by the prophet Ezekiel as one of the three most righteous people to ever live, Job was a very rich man who was tested by losing everything, including his family and health; however, his trust in God could not be shaken. He refused to curse God and was rewarded with twice as much as he lost. NASU, NKJV, *and* NIV *Chapters:* The book of Job.

Joel: (jō'əl, jō'el') *YHWH is God:* One Joel, the firstborn son of Samuel, was appointed as a judge over Israel with his brother Abijah. Another Joel, the son of Gad, was a chief, while a third, the son of Zichri, was an overseer. NASU, NKJV, *and* NIV *Chapters:* 1 Samuel 8; 1 Chronicles 5; Nehemiah 11; and the book of Joel.

¹²John: (jän) *YHWH is gracious:* One, the brother of James of Zebedee, was an Apostle. Another was a relative of Jesus. Nicknamed John the Baptist for his work, he taught that the Messiah's coming was near. When talking about John, Jesus himself said: "Assuredly, I say to you, among those born of women there has not risen one greater than John the Baptist;" (Matthew 11:11, NKJV). Another was one of Jesus' three closest apostles. NASU, NKJV, *and* NIV *Chapters:* Matthew 3, 4, 9–11, 14, 17, 21; Mark 1, 3, 5, 6, 9, 10, 13, 14; Luke 1, 3, 5–9, 22; the book of John; Acts 1, 3, 4, 8, 12, 13, 15; Galatians 2; the books of 1, 2, 3 John; and the book of Revelation.

*Jonah: (jō′nə) *dove:* As the son of Amittai the prophet, he too was a prophet, although a reluctant one. While fleeing the Lord's instructions to rebuke the city of Nineveh, Jonah took ship to Tarshish. While at sea, the Lord caused a great storm to scare the crew into throwing him overboard. He resided in the belly of a great fish for three days and nights before finally agreeing to follow God's will. He spoke the words of the Lord during the reign of King Jeroboam. NASU *and* NIV *Chapters:* 2 Kings 14; the book of Jonah; Matthew 12; and Luke 11. NKJV *Differences:* Add John 1 and 21 since it names another Jonah's son as the Apostle Peter.

Jonathan: (jän'ə thən) *YHWH has given:* The son of King Saul. Jonathan was best friends with soon-to-be King David. He was loyal, even saving David's life when Saul tried to kill him. A different Jonathan was Abiathar's son, the man who tried to usurp the throne from the elderly King David and his son Solomon. A third Jonathan, the nephew of David and Shimea's son, killed one of the giants from Gath and served in David's army. A fourth Jonathan, David's uncle, was a scribe who was noted for his great wisdom. Jonathan the son of Shagee the Hararite was one of King David's "mighty men." *Finally, another one became a priest of an idolatrous cult in the tribe of Dan. NASU, NKJV, *and* NIV *Chapters:* Judges 18; 1 Samuel 13, 14, 18–20, 23, 31; 2 Samuel 17, 21; 1 Kings 1; and 1 Chronicles 8, 10, 11, 20, and 27.

Joseph: (jō'zəf, jō'səf) *he will add:* A carpenter who was Jesus' earthly father. Another Joseph, the second to youngest son of Jacob, was his father's favorite child and was given a coat of many colors;

in fact, his brothers sold him into slavery because of envy. He was made the prime minister of Egypt after years of faithful service and successfully interpreting Pharaoh's dreams. A third Joseph was one of Jesus' physical brothers. Also, there was a rich man named Joseph, a disciple from Arimathea who collected Jesus' body from Pilate, wrapped it in clean linen, and laid the body in his new tomb, which was hewn out of stone. Finally, he rolled the stone over the entrance and left. NASU, NKJV, *and* NIV *Chapters:* Genesis 30, 33, 35, 37, 39–50; Exodus 1, 13; Joshua 24; 1 Chronicles 2; Matthew 1, 2, 13, 27; Mark 15; Luke 1–3, 23; John 19; and Acts 7.

Joshua: (jäsh′yoo ə, jäsh′oo ə) *YHWH is salvation:* The son of Nun, A great military man, and faithful follower of God, Joshua was a servant of Moses and one of the two spies who reported favorably of conquering the Promised Land. Since Moses couldn't enter the Promised Land, he asked God to appoint a leader for Israel. The Lord chose Joshua, saying: "Take Joshua the son of Nun, a man in whom is the Spirit, and lay your hand on him; and have him stand before Eleazar the priest and before all the congregation, and commission him in their sight. You shall put some of your authority on him, in order that all the congregation of the sons of Israel may obey him. Moreover, he shall stand before Eleazar the priest, who shall inquire for him by the judgment of the Urim before the LORD. At his command they shall go out and at his command they shall come in, both he and the sons of Israel with him, even all the congregation" (Numbers 27:18–21, NASU). Another Joshua, the son of Jehozadak, was a high priest. There's also a Joshua listed in the genealogy of Jesus. NASU *and* NIV *Chapters:* Exodus 17, 24, 32, 33; Numbers 11, 13, 14, 26, 27, 32, 34; Deuteronomy 1, 3, 31, 32, 34; the book of Joshua; Judges 1, 2; 1 Kings 16; 1 Chronicles 7; Haggai 1, 2; Zechariah 3, 6; and Luke 3. NKJV *Differences:* Drop Luke 3 since it uses another for the genealogy line.

Josiah: (jō sī'ə, jō zī'ə) *YHWH supports:* A king of Judah at eight years old, Josiah reigned as king for thirty-one years. He restored God's temple at age twenty-six and soon became the second most famous king of Israel; moreover, he is listed in the genealogy of Jesus. NASU, NKJV, *and* NIV *Chapters:* 1 Kings 13; 2 Kings 21–23; 1 Chronicles 3; 2 Chronicles 33–36; and Matthew 1.

Judah: (joo′də) *praised:* A son of Jacob, he convinced his brothers not to kill their father's favorite, Joseph, and instead sell him into slavery. He's listed in the genealogy of Jesus and formed the tribe of Judah with God's blessing. NASU, NKJV, *and* NIV *Chapters:* Genesis 29, 35, 37, 38, 43, 44, 46, 49; Exodus 1; 1 Chronicles 2; and Luke 3.

Judas: (joo′dəs) *praise:* One Judas was the physical brother of Jesus. **12 Another, one of the twelve Apostles and the son of Simon Iscariot, betrayed Jesus with a kiss. He was said to have stolen money for himself out of the traveling funds for Jesus and the twelve apostles. 12 A third, the son of James, was a faithful Apostle. He was comforted, loved, and taught by Jesus; furthermore, he helped start and maintain the churches after Jesus ascended into heaven. NASU, NKJV, *and* NIV *Chapters:* Matthew 10, 13, 26, 27; Mark 3, 6, 14; Luke 6, 22; John 6, 12–14, 18; and Acts 1, 5, 9, and 15.

Jude: (jood) *Jude is short for Judas:* A physical brother of Jesus who didn't believe until after the resurrection. NASU, NKJV, *and* NIV *Chapters:* The book of Jude.

L

Levi: (lē′vī′) *attached:* The third son of Jacob, who started the tribe of Levi with God's blessing. Levi and his brother Simon snuck into the city of Shechem, killed every male there, and rescued their sister, Dinah, who was taken and violated by Shechem, the son of Hamor. Another Levi, who was a tax collector named Matthew, was an Apostle of Jesus; consequently, he wrote the book of Matthew. NASU, NKJV, *and* NIV *Chapters:* Genesis 29, 34, 35, 46, 49; Exodus 1; Mark 2; and Luke 3, 5.

Linus: (lī nəs) *flax, interweaved:* In a letter written by the Apostle Paul to Timothy, Linus is one of four people personally mentioned. This indicates that he was well known and befriended in at least two regional churches. NASU, NKJV, *and* NIV *Chapters:* 2 Timothy 4.

Luke: (look) *illumination:* A lifelong friend, supporter, and helper of Paul, he was a gentle doctor who compiled a historical account of Jesus' life and works. NASU, NKJV, *and* NIV *Chapters:* The book of Luke; Colossians 4; 2 Timothy 4; and Philemon.

M

Mark: (märk) *hammer:* Also called John, he was a helper and friend of Peter. He assisted Paul and Barnabas on a missionary trip but quit in the middle of it when they were in Pamphylia. When the second trip was planned, Paul and Barnabas got into a fight about bringing Mark along and parted ways; therefore, Paul went with Silas and Barnabas went with Mark. As a credible witness to the Romans, Mark wrote the story of Jesus' life and works. NASU, NKJV, *and* NIV *Chapters:* the book of Mark; Acts 12, 15; Colossians 4; 2 Timothy 4; Philemon 24; and 1 Peter 5.

[12]**Matthew:** (math′yoo′) *gift of YHWH:* A Jewish tax gatherer. When asked, Matthew immediately left his very wealthy job to follow Jesus and later became one of the twelve apostles. He wrote to the Jewish people about the life of Jesus and the new covenant of God. NASU, NKJV, *and* NIV *Chapters:* the book of Matthew; Mark 3; Luke 6; and Acts 1.

Mica: (mī′kə) *same as Micah/Michael:* One Mica is listed in the tribe of Benjamin as a great-grandson of King Saul. His father was Mephibosheth, and his grandfather was Jonathan. Another one, a Levite, was a professional singer for the house of God. NASU, NKJV, *and* NIV *Chapters:* 2 Samuel; 1 Chronicles 9; and Nehemiah 10, 11.

Micah: (mī′kə) *no one is like YHWH:* One, from the hill country of Ephraim, lived with his mother and hired a Levite to become their household priest for room and board, a set of clothes, and ten pieces of silver a year. Another, Micah of Moresheth, was a prophet who received the word of the Lord during the reign of Kings Jotham, Ahaz, and Hezekiah of Judah. NASU, NKJV, *and* NIV *Chapters:* Judges 17, 18; 1 Chronicles 5, 8; Jeremiah 26; and the book of Micah.

Michael: (mī′kəl) *no one is like God:* One, from the tribe of Asher, had his son Sethur chosen to spy out the Promise Land for Moses. Also, two are listed in the genealogy of Reuben, one in the priestly genealogy of Levi, one in the genealogy of Issachar, and one in the genealogy of Benjamin. Another Michael, who came from Manasseh, is listed as one of King David's "mighty men." Jehoshaphat king of Israel had a son named Michael. Finally, there's Michael the Archangel. When the devil wanted to defile the body of Moses, Michael protected it by saying, "The Lord rebuke you!" (Jude 9). This archangel is possibly the same "chief prince" who came to help Daniel when he was by the bank of the great river Tigris. In Revelation, Michael and his angels are seen waging war and defeating the great dragon (the devil), thereby expelling him and his angels from heaven. NASU, NKJV, *and* NIV *Chapters:* Numbers 13; 1 Chronicles 5–8, 12, 27; 2 Chronicles 21; Daniel 10, 12; Jude 9; and Revelation 12.

*Moses: (mō′zəz, mō′zəs) *drawn out:* A man with stage fright who was not good at public speaking; nevertheless, God selected him for many tasks throughout his life. Moses was chosen to perform many signs (plagues), forcing the Egyptians to release the Hebrews from slavery. He failed God when he struck a rock instead of speaking to it as instructed; consequently, he was not allowed into the Promised Land because of this. Instead he was led up a mountain to spend the rest of his days under God's care. NASU, NKJV, *and* NIV *Chapters:* Exodus 2–20, 24, 32–36, 39, 40; Leviticus 8–10, 24; Numbers 1, 3, 4, 7–17, 20, 21, 25–27, 29–34; Deuteronomy 1, 4, 5, 27, 29, 31–34; Joshua 1; 1 Chronicles 6, 23; Psalm 90; Matthew 17; Mark 9; Luke 9; Acts 3, 7; Romans 10; Hebrews 11; Jude 9; and Revelation 15.

N

Nathan: (nā′thən) *gift or giver:* One, who is listed in the genealogy of Jesus, was a son of King David and born in Jerusalem. A second one, who was a prophet and advisor to David, worked as a spiritual advisor by relaying God's messages to the Jewish people. Another Nathan is listed in the thirty seven "mighty men" of King David's personal guard. *The fourth, a priest, was listed with the offenders who had taken foreign wives. NASU, NKJV, *and* NIV *Chapters:* 2 Samuel 5, 7, 12, 23; 1 Kings 1, 4; 1 Chronicles 2, 3, 11, 14, 17, 29; 2 Chronicles 9, 29; Ezra 8, 10; Psalm 51; Zechariah 12; and Luke 3.

Nathanael: (nə than′yəl, nə than′ē əl) *God has given:* He was a faithful follower of God who was eagerly awaiting the prophesies of old to be fulfilled. When Jesus was traveling and gathering disciples to himself, Philip went to get Nathanael, explaining that the Messiah had finally been found in Jesus of Nazareth. At first, Nathanael was skeptical and, with the humor of good friends, replied, "Can anything good come out of Nazareth?" (John 1:46, NKJV). As they were approaching him, Jesus looked at Nathanael and said, "Behold, an Israelite indeed, in whom there is no deceit!" (John 1:47, NASU). It took only two sentences for Jesus to convince Nathanael that he was the Son of God; consequently, Nathanael became a disciple and good friend to all the faithful. He was in the boat where Jesus revealed himself after the resurrection. NASU, NKJV, *and* NIV *Chapters:* John 1 and 21.

Nicolas: (nik′ə ləs) *victory of the people:* A proselyte from Antioch and one of the seven original deacons. Nicolas was one of seven men of good reputation, full of the spirit and of wisdom chosen to serve the Hellenistic (Greek-speaking) Jewish widows a daily portion of food. NASU, NKJV, *and* NIV *Chapters:* Acts 6.

⁺⁺Noah: (nō′ə) *rest, comfort:* A man of great faith who is listed in the genealogy of Jesus, Noah was faithful to God when the rest of the world wasn't. Through much ridicule, it took him around 120 years to build the ark with his family. God chose Noah, his wife, and his sons' families to repopulate the earth after he destroyed everything with a flood. NASU, NKJV, *and* NIV *Chapters:* Genesis 5–10; 1 Chronicles 1; Luke 3; Hebrews 11; and 2 Peter 2.

O

Obadiah: (ō′bə dī′ə) *servant of YHWH:* He worked as a servant of King Ahab. Obadiah was able to save one hundred prophets by hiding them in a cave and providing them with food and water. Another Obadiah was a descendant of King David. A third was a clan chieftain in the tribe of Issachar. A fourth was one of King David's "mighty men." NASU, NKJV, *and* NIV *Chapters:* 1 Kings 18; 1 Chronicles 3, 12; 2 Chronicles 17, 34; Ezra 8; Nehemiah 10, 12; and the book of Obadiah.

P

Paul: (pôl) *humble:* Under the name Saul, he started off persecuting Christians because he thought they were a sect against Mosaic Law. Later, as he was traveling by the outskirts of Damascus, the Lord spoke with him, removing his sight and directing him to enter the city. After three days, the Lord sent Ananias to restore his sight. Ananias laid his hands on him and said, "Brother Saul, the Lord Jesus, who appeared to you on the road as you came, has sent me that you may receive your sight and be filled with the Holy Spirit" (Acts 9:17, NKJV). Saul, later known as Paul, was immediately baptized and converted to Christianity, becoming one of the hardest-working missionaries of that time; in fact, he has written many of the books in the Bible. NASU, NKJV, *and* NIV *Chapters:* Acts 9, 13–28; the books of: Romans, 1 and 2 Corinthians, Galatians, Ephesians, Philippians, Colossians, 1 and 2 Thessalonians, 1 and 2 Timothy, Titus, and Philemon.

¹²**Peter:** (pēt′ər) *stone:* His first name was Simon before Jesus renamed him Cephas, which is translated as Peter. He was a fisherman with his brother Andrew before they became two of Jesus' twelve apostles. He was a follower with great faith, which allowed him to walk on the water with Jesus for a little while, before succumbing to his fear and sinking. When Jesus changed Simon's name to Cephas, it was a prelude of his plan for him. This plan, and the meaning of his new name, was revealed when Jesus told him, "I also say to you that you are Peter, and upon this rock I will build My church; and the gates of Hades will not overpower it. I will give you the keys of the kingdom of heaven; and whatever you bind on earth shall have been bound in heaven, and whatever you loose on earth shall have been loosed in heaven" (Matthew 16:18–19, NASU). NASU, NKJV, *and* NIV *Chapters:* Matthew 4, 10, 14–19, 26; Mark 3, 5, 8–11, 13, 14, 16; Luke 5, 6, 8, 9, 12, 18, 22,

24; John 1, 6, 13, 18, 20, 21; Acts 1–5, 8–12, 15; Galatians 1, 2; and the books of 1 and 2 Peter.

*Philip: (fil'ip) *friend of horses:* One, the tetrarch of the region of Ituraea and Trachonitis, was the brother of Herod, the man who beheaded John the Baptist. 12 Another, from Bethsaida, was one of the twelve Apostles and the man who informed his friend Nathanael that the Messiah had been found in Jesus of Nazareth. A third Philip was an evangelist and one of the original seven deacons who were listed as men of good reputation, full of the spirit and of wisdom. They were chosen to serve the Hellenistic (Greek-speaking) Jewish widows a daily portion of food. NASU, NKJV, *and* NIV *Chapters:* Matthew 10, 14; Mark 3, 6; Luke 3, 6; John 1, 6, 12, 14; and Acts 1, 6, 8, and 21.

R

Ram: (ram) *exalted:* Nothing was written of Ram other than the fact that he was listed in the genealogy of Jesus and King David. NASU, NKJV, *and* NIV *Chapters:* Ruth 4; 1 Chronicles 2; and Matthew 1.

Reuben: (roo′bən) *behold, a son:* The firstborn son of Jacob and Leah. He was the only brother who wanted to help Joseph escape. Reuben planned to secretly rescue him from the empty cistern when the other brothers had left; however, his plan failed when they sold Joseph into slavery behind his back. NASU, NKJV, *and* NIV *Chapters:* Genesis 29, 30, 35, 37, 42, 46, 48, 49; Exodus 1, 6; 1 Chronicles 2, 5.

Rufus: (roo′fəs) *red-haired:* His father was Simon, the man from Cyrene who was pressed into the service of carrying Jesus' cross part of the way. Paul sends greetings to another Rufus, "a choice man in the Lord," to whom he was friends with. NASU, NKJV, *and* NIV *Chapters:* Mark 15; Romans 16.

S

Samuel: (sam′yoo əl, sam′yool) *God has heard:* One was a leader in the tribe of Simeon. The Lord appointed him to apportion part of the Promised Land for his tribe's inheritance. Another, the son of Elkanah and Hannah, was named Samuel by his mother "Because I have asked him of the LORD" (1 Samuel 1:20, NASU). He was dedicated to the Lord for service in the temple; as such, he was given to the care of the priest Eli just after Hannah had weaned him from nursing. This Samuel rose in stature and favor both with the Lord and men. The Lord called Samuel to the service of a prophet when he was still just a boy. This event in his story has many wonderful intricacies and can be found in 1 Samuel 3:1–21. Samuel also worked as a Judge over Israel. When he was old and ready to appoint his sons as judges, the people asked instead for a king to judge them. NASU, NKJV, *and* NIV *Chapters:* The books of 1 and 2 Samuel; 1 Chronicles 6, 7, 9, 11, 26, 29; and Acts 13.

*Saul: (sôl) *asked for, prayed for:* He was good looking, taller than most men, and a farmer. He had no desire for power and was anointed king against his wishes; however, later on in his rule, he lost favor with God and was replaced by David. Another Saul was the man who started off violently persecuting the church before the Lord converted him and changed his name to Paul. NASU *and* NIV *Chapters:* 1 Samuel 9–11, 13–29, 31; 1 Chronicles 8–10; and Acts 7–9, 11–13, 22, and 26. NKJV*:* Add Genesis 36 and 1 Chronicles 1 and 5 since the other two versions use the spelling Shaul.

Seth: (seth) *appointed:* The third son of Adam and Eve. Eve said that Seth was a gift from God to replace Abel, who was slain by his brother. Seth looked very much like his father, Adam. He was 105 before he had a son of his own, whom he named Enosh. Overall, Seth lived for 912 years. NASU, NKJV, *and* NIV *Chapters:* Genesis 4, 5; 1 Chronicles 1; and Luke 3.

[12]**Simon:** (sī′mən) *he has heard:* The apostle of Jesus who was known as Peter. 12 A different Simon, also an apostle, was called "Simon the Zealot." He left a sect to follow Jesus. Another, who helped carry Jesus' cross, was the father of Rufus and Alexander. Also, there was the Simon who was the father of Judas Iscariot, Jesus' betrayer. **Finally, there was a magician named Simon from Samaria who wanted the power of the Holy Spirit. He tried to buy the power from Simon Peter, for his own ends, and was harshly rebuked. NASU, NKJV, *and* NIV *Chapters:* Matthew 4, 10, 13, 16, 17, 26, 27; Mark 1, 3, 6, 14, 15; Luke 5–7, 22–24; John 1, 6, 13, 18, 20, 21; Acts 1, 8–11, 15; and the books of 1 and 2 Peter.

Stephen: (stē′vən) *crown:* As a martyr of Christianity, he was filled with the Holy Spirit and spread the gospel of Jesus to many. He was named one of the seven original deacons to serve the Hellenistic (Greek-speaking) Jewish widows a daily portion of food, and he performed great wonders and signs among the people. NASU, NKJV, *and* NIV *Chapters:* Acts 6–8, 11, and 22.

T

12Thaddaeus: (thad′aē əs, tha daē′əs) *heart:* As one of the twelve apostles whom Jesus chose, there was little written of him. When the apostles are named, Thaddaeus, sometimes called Judas the son of James, comes up at the end of the list. This possibly shows that he played a lesser role compared to the others; nevertheless, Jesus chose Thaddaeus as a traveling companion and one of twelve men to spread the gospel of Christianity. Nothing bad was written about him or his work for the Lord. NASU, NKJV, *and* NIV *Chapters:* Matthew 10 and Mark 3.

12Thomas: (täm′əs) *twin:* One of Jesus' twelve apostles. Thomas was known as Didymus (Twin) because he always strained to copy Jesus in every way. This is a good example of the friendly, teasing, and joking life the apostles shared with Jesus and one another. He's remembered as "Doubting Thomas" because he wouldn't believe in Jesus' resurrection until he saw and felt the wounds in Jesus' side and hands. NASU, NKJV, *and* NIV *Chapters:* Matthew 10; Mark 3; Luke 6; John 11, 14, 20, 21; and Acts 1.

Timothy: (tim′ə thē) *honoring God:* A newly-converted disciple from the town of Lystra. Timothy was young, timid, sickly, and sensitive. He was also a faithful Christian who genuinely cared for others. Paul, who baptized and circumcised him, came to love him as a son. He performed many works by delivering letters, helping Christians, and staying at congregations to strengthen them. NASU, NKJV, *and* NIV *Chapters:* Acts 16–20; Romans 16; 1 Corinthians 4, 16; 2 Corinthians 1; Philippians 1, 2; Colossians 1; 1 Thessalonians 1, 3; 2 Thessalonians 1; the books of 1 and 2 Timothy; Philemon 1; and Hebrews 13.

U

Uriah: (yoo rī′ə) *YHWH is my light:* A faithful and true warrior who was betrayed by King David. While Uriah was at war, David lay with his wife. Then the king ordered him to the front lines to be abandoned and killed, thereby getting Uriah out of the way so his wife would be free to remarry. God avenged Uriah for King David's treachery. Another Uriah was a priest whose prophecies against Judah were very stern; therefore, King Jehoiakim sent men to track him throughout the city and even to Egypt. Uriah was finally captured there, returned to the king, and killed. NASU, NKJV, *and* NIV *Chapters:* 2 Samuel 11, 12, 23; 1 Kings 15; 2 Kings 16; 1 Chronicles 11; Ezra 8; Nehemiah 3, 8; Isaiah 8; Jeremiah 26; and Matthew 1.

Z

Zacchaeus/Zaccheus: (za kē əs) *pure:* He was a wealthy tax gatherer who gained his riches by cheating people. Zacchaeus, being too short to see over the crowd, climbed a tree to see Jesus walk by; consequently, upon seeing him, Jesus called him down, saying he would eat at Zacchaeus's house. Zacchaeus repented and made restitution to those he stole from. As a result, Jesus replied by saying, "Today salvation has come to this house" (Luke 19:9, NKJV). NASU, NKJV, *and* NIV *Chapters:* Luke 19.

*Zacharias/ Zachariah: (zak'ə rī'yəs) *YHWH remembers:* The father of John the Baptist, Zacharias was an elderly priest who served in the temple two weeks a year. Given the honor of burning the incense, he was in the sanctuary when the angel Gabriel came and told him that he and his wife, Elizabeth, would have a son.

Zacharias wasn't allowed to speak until the child was born because he didn't believe Gabriel; in fact, he and his wife were too old to normally have children since they were around one hundred years old at the time. NASU, NKJV, *and* NIV *Chapters:* Luke 1 and 3.

Names for Girls

Then God said to Abraham, "As for Sarai your wife, you shall not call her name Sarai, but Sarah shall be her name. I will bless her, and indeed I will give you a son by her. Then I will bless her, and she shall be a mother of nations; kings of peoples will come from her."

Genesis 17:15–16 (NASU)

** People continually failing, strongly against God, or not Christian.

* People who failed God and were punished in a severe way.

A

Abigail: (ab′ə gāl′) *my father is joy:* She was a smart, beautiful, and resourceful woman. When her first husband, Nabal, offended King David, she went in secret to intercept the solders the king had sent for revenge. She convinced them to wait and spared her husband and land by pacifying David with an apology and gifts. She married the king after her husband's death. Another Abigail was King David's sister. NASU, NKJV, *and* NIV *Chapters:* 1 Samuel 25, 27, 30; 2 Samuel 2, 3, 17; and 1 Chronicles 2, 3.

Anna: (an′ə) *favor, grace:* She was the daughter of Phanuel and a prophetess, who was widowed after only seven years. While waiting for the presentation of baby Jesus, Anna spent most of her life in prayer and fasting at the temple. At eighty-four years old, when she finally saw Jesus, she passionately rejoiced that God had allowed her to live that long. NASU, NKJV, *and* NIV *Chapters:* Luke 2.

B

Bernice: (bər nēs′, bur′nis) *bringing victory:* Little is written of Bernice, although her brother was King Agrippa. When Paul was held captive at Caesarea under Festus, Bernice and her brother went there to visit. At the request of Agrippa, Festus held a repeat trial so the king and his sister could hear Paul speak. Neither of them cared for Christianity, even though Paul almost convinced the King to convert. They did agree that the charges against Paul were false, although they had to send him to Caesar because he requested it at the beginning of the proceedings. NASU, NKJV, *and* NIV *Chapters:* Acts 25 and 26.

C

Chloe: (klō′ē) *green shoot:* It's unclear if Chloe was a Christian; however, her slaves reported dissention in the Corinthian church so that the problem could be solved before it festered. With this forewarning, the Apostle Paul addresses the problem of divisions in the church in his letter to Corinth. NASU, NKJV, *and* NIV *Chapters:* 1 Corinthians 1.

Claudia: (klô′dē ə) *crippled:* A friend of Paul, Claudia helped by visiting and caring for Paul when he was imprisoned in Rome. Paul writes of her and relays her greetings in his letter to Timothy. NASU, NKJV, *and* NIV *Chapters:* 2 Timothy 4.

D

Deborah: (deb′ə rə, deb′rə) *bee:* One was Rebekah's nurse. She passed away at Bethel after the family had just traveled there. She was buried under an oak tree, which they named Allon-bacuth in her honor. Another Deborah was a prophetess and the only Jewish female Judge. She would sit under the palm tree of Deborah, where people would come for many of her judgments. After she summoned Barak, the son of Abinoamand, and told him of the Lord's wishes, she led him and ten thousand troops through a victorious war with the army of Jabin. NASU, NKJV, *and* NIV *Chapters:* Genesis 35; Judges 4, 5.

Dinah: (dī′nə) *judged:* The daughter of Jacob, Dinah was so beautiful that when she went into town to visit the city girls, she was captured and violated by Prince Shechem, the Canaanite. When he asked for her hand in marriage, her brothers found out that he had captured and laid with her by force. They repaid the defilement of their sister by sneaking into the city, killing every male, and rescuing Dinah. NASU, NKJV, *and* NIV *Chapters:* Genesis 30, 34, and 46.

E

Elizabeth: (ē liz′ə bəth, i liz′ə bəth) *my God is an oath:* Well beyond her childbearing years, she was the mother of John the Baptist. Elizabeth was in her sixth month of pregnancy when she comforted her younger cousin Mary. During this meeting, her unborn baby leapt for joy, when Mary greeted her. After that, Elizabeth told of her visit from an angel foretelling of her child. Likewise, Mary told of her visit from an angel, explaining her pregnancy of the baby Jesus, whom she would have as a virgin. By sharing their extraordinary pregnancies, they lived with and supported each other for three months. NASU, NKJV, *and* NIV *Chapters:* Luke 1.

Esther: (es′tər) *star:* Originally named Hadassah, Esther was a very beautiful woman. As an orphan, Esther was raised by her cousin Mordecai. She was chosen to replace Queen Vashti as the Persian queen of King Ahasuerus because she was so beautiful. NASU, NKJV, *and* NIV *Chapters:* the book of Esther.

*Eve: (ēv) *to live:* The first woman and mother of all. Eve was handmade by God from Adam's rib. After the serpent tricked her, she was cursed with pain in childbirth when she ate of the forbidden fruit. This was very unfortunate since she then had the job of populating the earth. The Bible doesn't say how long Eve lived, although her husband, Adam, lived to be 930. It is assumed that she would have lived to a like age. NASU, NKJV, *and* NIV *Chapters:* Genesis 3, 4; 1 Timothy 2.

H

Hannah: (han′ə) *favor, grace:* Her husband was Elkanah. As was normal for the time and culture, Elkanah had two wives; the other of which was a woman named Peninnah. Now Peninnah had children, but since Hannah was barren, Peninnah would "provoke her bitterly to irritate her, because the Lord had closed her womb" (1 Samuel 1:6, NASU). This happened for years, causing Hannah to weep bitterly and refuse to eat. Finally, when she could take it no more, she prayed to the Lord and promised her child to him if he would only open her womb. The Lord answered her prayer and she bore Samuel, the great prophet and judge over Israel. Other than Jesus, it is likely possible that Samuel was the only *boy* to serve in the temple. Hannah was a devout mother and specially made a little robe every year for Samuel to use in his work. Later, Hannah had another three boys and two girls of her own. NASU, NKJV, *and* NIV *Chapters:* 1 Samuel 1 and 2.

J

Joanna: (jō an′ə) *YHWH is gracious:* Jesus healed her of sickness and/or evil spirits. Joanna was a woman of means, a devoted follower, and helped support Jesus and the twelve apostles. She was one of the women who went to Jesus' tomb to anoint his body with ointments and spices; however, when they got there and found the tomb empty, an angel told them of Jesus' resurrection. NASU, NKJV, *and* NIV *Chapters:* Luke 8 and 24.

Judith: (joo′dith) *woman from Judea:* Her father was Beeri the Hittite, and her husband was Esau. She married him when he was forty; however, their marriage brought only grief to Isaac and Rebekah. NASU, NKJV, *and* NIV *Chapters:* Genesis 26.

Julia: (jool′yə, joo′lē ə) *soft:* In a letter that the Apostle Paul wrote to all the saints in Rome, Julia is mentioned as worthy of greetings and a holy kiss from the churches. NASU, NKJV, *and* NIV *Chapters:* Romans 16.

L

Leah: (lē'ə) *weary:* She wasn't very beautiful, so her father tricked her younger sister's husband-to-be, Jacob, into marring her. He accomplished this by switching the sisters on the wedding night, covering Leah's face with the wedding dress and placing her as the bride at her sister's wedding. Leah and Jacob still had many children together, though, and the three of them got along well as a family. NASU, NKJV, *and* NIV *Chapters:* Genesis 29–31, 33, and 49.

Lois: (lō'is) *more desirable, better:* She was the mother of Eunice and grandmother of Timothy. Paul praises her for having sincere faith and gives her credit for passing it on to her daughter and grandson. NASU, NKJV, *and* NIV *Chapters:* 2 Timothy 1.

Lydia: (lid'ē ə) *from Lydia:* She was originally from the town of Thyatira but was living in the district of Macedonia, in the prominent city of Philippi, when Paul found, converted, and baptized her and her household. Lydia sold purple dye, was well to do, and was a backbone member of the congregation at Philippi. NASU, NKJV, *and* NIV *Chapters:* Acts 16.

M

Martha: (mär′thə) *lady of the house:* The older sister of Mary, the sister of Lazarus, and a friend of Jesus. She's known for worrying about household chores and serving guests instead of listening to Jesus teach. The Bible states that Jesus loved Martha, Mary, and Lazarus, so when their brother fell sick and died, he came to their town and raised Lazarus from the dead. NASU, NKJV, *and* NIV *Chapters:* Luke 10; John 11, 12.

Mary: (mer′ē, mar′ē) *possibly meaning beloved:* Mary was selected by God, out of all women, to be Jesus' mother. Also, there was Jesus' Aunt Mary, the wife of Clopas, who was one of the women who stood vigil at the crucifixion. Another Mary was Martha's sister and a beloved friend of Jesus. Mary Magdalene and a fifth Mary, the mother of James and Joseph, followed Jesus for a time and helped take care of him. They were two of the women who met the angel at the tomb after the resurrection. A fourth was the wealthy mother of John, who was also called Mark. She used her house, which had a courtyard, as a church building. This is the building where the servant girl, Rhoda, forgot to open the gate for Peter after the angel let him escape from jail. Instead, she ran to the house excitedly, telling everyone that he was at the front gate. NASU, NKJV, *and* NIV *Chapters:* Matthew 1, 2, 13, 27, 28; Mark 6, 15, 16; Luke 1, 2, 8, 10, 24; John 11, 12, 19, 20; and Acts 1, 12, and 16.

Miriam: (mir′ē əm) *possibly meaning sea of bitterness:* A woman prophetess and the older sister of Moses, Miriam helped save Moses when he was a baby, by watching over him from a distance when he was floating in a basket on the Nile. The Pharaoh's daughter found him and took the baby as her own. In Micah 6:4 the Lord honors her and her brothers by saying to the Jews: "I sent before you Moses, Aaron, and Miriam" (NKJV). NASU, NKJV, *and* NIV *Chapters:* Exodus 15; Numbers 12, 20, 26; 1 Chronicles 4, 6; and Micah 6.

N

Naomi: (nā ō′mē, nī-, nā′ə mī′) *pleasantness:* After fleeing the famine in Bethlehem, her husband, Elimelech, and two sons, Mahlon and Chilion, died. After this, the elderly Naomi returned to her homeland with her daughter-in-law Ruth, who would not leave her alone and helpless. She was faithfully helped by Ruth, and they both prospered. NASU, NKJV, *and* NIV *Chapters:* Ruth 1–4.

P

Phoebe: (fē′bē) *bright, pure:* She was a servant and helper to the church in Cenchrea. So much so that Paul writes of her to all the faithful in Rome, saying: "…receive her in the Lord in a manner worthy of the saints, and that you help her in whatever matter she may have need of you; for she herself has also been a helper of many, and of myself as well" (Romans 16:2, NASU). NASU, NKJV, *and* NIV *Chapters:* Romans 16.

Prisca: (pri əa) More commonly Priscilla (pri sil′ə) *ancient:* She was a great and faithful Christian. Prisca is listed before her husband two different times in the Bible. Considering the different positions accorded to men and women at the time, this implies her astonishing social position and work for the church. NASU, NKJV, *and* NIV *Chapters:* Acts 18; Romans 16; 1 Corinthians 16; and 2 Timothy 4.

R

Rachel: (rā′chəl) *ewe, female sheep:* Rachel was such a stunning shepherdess that Jacob, upon seeing her, helped her to water her entire flock, kissed her (the only romantic kiss mentioned in the Bible), and then wept. A month later, he ended up working for her father for fourteen years just to receive her hand in marriage. NASU, NKJV, *and* NIV *Chapters:* Genesis 29–31, 33, 35, 46, and 48.

*Rebekah: (ri bek′ə) *to snare:* She was very beautiful, and the Lord chose her to marry Issac. She helped her younger son, Jacob, to cheat his older brother, Esau; furthermore, she helped him escape his brother's wrath by sending him to her brother, Laban, who lived in Haran. NASU, NKJV, *and* NIV *Chapters:* Genesis 22, 24–28, and 49.

Rhoda: (rō′də) *rose:* She was a servant of Mary, the mother of Mark. Rhoda answered the front gate door when Peter, who had escaped from prison with the help of an angel, knocked. She was so excited that she forgot to let him in, ran to the house, and excitedly told the others that he was at the front gate. NASU, NKJV, *and* NIV *Chapters:* Acts 12.

Ruth: (rooth) *friend:* After her first husband died, she "adopted" her elderly mother-in-law, Naomi. After traveling to Naomi's hometown of Bethlehem, Ruth then met her second husband, Boaz, who was a wealthy man. Ruth is listed in the genealogy of Jesus and King David. NASU, NKJV, *and* NIV *Chapters:* the book of Ruth; Matthew 1.

S

Sarah: (ser'ə, sar'ə) *princess:* She was extremely beautiful. Even after Sarah was sixty-six years old, her husband, Abraham, was afraid that an Egyptian would kill him to marry her. She had no children until God blessed her with pregnancy when she was in her nineties. NASU, NKJV, *and* NIV *Chapters:* Genesis 17, 18, 20, 21, 23, 49; Hebrews 11; and 1 Peter 3.

Susanna: (soo zan'ə) *lily:* She was a faithful ministering woman. Susanna followed Jesus for a time after being healed of either a sickness and/or demon possession. She contributed to the support of Jesus and the twelve out of her private means. NASU, NKJV, *and* NIV *Chapters:* Luke 8.

Tabitha: (tab′i thə) *gazelle:* A disciple from Joppa, She was wealthy, much loved, and best known for her many acts of charity. Along with giving money to the needy, Tabitha made clothes for the poor. After her death, members of the church desperately went to Peter for help. He responded by raising her from the dead. NASU, NKJV, *and* NIV *Chapters:* Acts 9.

About the Author

David Brown was born and raised in northern Minnesota. He attended church while growing up and decided at age eighteen to travel the country, seeking God and the answers to life. He spent over nine years traveling—from Hollywood to Norfolk, Virginia. Today he resides back in his hometown.

e|LIVE

---

listen|imagine|view|experience

AUDIO BOOK DOWNLOAD INCLUDED WITH THIS BOOK!

In your hands you hold a complete digital entertainment package. Besides purchasing the paper version of this book, this book includes a free download of the audio version of this book. Simply use the code listed below when visiting our website. Once downloaded to your computer, you can listen to the book through your computer's speakers, burn it to an audio CD or save the file to your portable music device (such as Apple's popular iPod) and listen on the go!

How to get your free audio book digital download:

1. Visit www.tatepublishing.com and click on the e|LIVE logo on the home page.
2. Enter the following coupon code:
   6171-66c2-c0b8-e6b2-398f-5933-013a-2d78
3. Download the audio book from your e|LIVE digital locker and begin enjoying your new digital entertainment package today!